W9-CZW-645

THE SCIENCE OF
NUTRITION

WHY WE NEED
MINERALS

By James Bow

Crabtree Publishing Company

www.crabtreebooks.com

Crabtree Publishing Company

www.crabtreebooks.com

Author: James Bow
Publishing plan research and development:
  Sean Charlebois, Reagan Miller
Editors: Sarah Eason, Nick Hunter, Lynn Peppas
Proofreaders: Robyn Hardyman, Kathy Middleton
Project coordinator: Kathy Middleton
Design: Calcium
Photo Research: Susannah Jayes
Print coordinator: Katherine Berti
Production coordinator and prepress technician:
  Ken Wright
Series consultant: Julie Negrin

Picture credits:
Public Health Image Library: CDC/ Dr Lyle Conrad 29,
  Jean Roy 15
Shutterstock: cover, 1000 words 11, Apollofoto 4, Yuri
  Arcurs 31, Andrey Armayagov 37, Ayakovlev.com 40,
  Anastasia Bobrova 14, Nadezhda Bolotina 27, Christo 10,
  Lucian Coman 24, Ron Dale 7, Phil Date 12, 16, 23, Fenton
  28–29, Marie C. Fields 13, Iakov Filimonov 42, Mike
  Flippo 25, Blaj Gabriel 39, Gravicapa 20, James Hoenstine
  21, Imcsike 35, Eric Isselée 9, 21, Jannoon028 30, Nataly
  Lukhanina 8, Piotr Marcinski 18, MonkeyBusines Images
  22, Fokin Oleg 6, Paul Prescott 34–35, StockLite 43,
  Tatjana Strelkova 36, Tihis 32–33, Wavebreakmedia ltd
  38–39, Ivonne Wierink 41, YanLev 26

Library and Archives Canada Cataloguing in Publication

Bow, James, 1972-
    Why we need minerals / James Bow.

(The science of nutrition)
Includes index.
Issued also in electronic format.
ISBN 978-0-7787-1688-4 (bound).--ISBN 978-0-7787-1695-2 (pbk.)

        1. Minerals in human nutrition--Juvenile literature.
I. Title. II. Series: Science of nutrition (St. Catharines, Ont.)

QP533.B69 2011   j612'.01524   C2011-900207-8

Library of Congress Cataloging-in-Publication Data

Bow, James.
    Why we need minerals / James Bow.
        p. cm. -- (The science of nutrition)
    Includes index.
    ISBN 978-0-7787-1695-2 (pbk. : alk. paper) -- ISBN 978-0-7787-1688-4
    (reinforced library binding : alk. paper) -- ISBN 978-1-4271-9679-8
    (electronic (pdf))
    1. Minerals in human nutrition--Juvenile literature. I. Title. II.
    Series.

    QP533.B69 2011
    612'.01524--dc22

                                                    2010052767

Crabtree Publishing Company

Printed in the U.S.A./022011/CJ20101228

www.crabtreebooks.com   1-800-387-7650

Published in Canada
Crabtree Publishing
616 Welland Ave.
St. Catharines, Ontario
L2M 5V6

Published in the United States
Crabtree Publishing
PMB 59051
350 Fifth Avenue, 59th Floor
New York, New York 10118

Published in the United Kingdom
Crabtree Publishing
Maritime House
Basin Road North, Hove
BN41 1WR

Published in Australia
Crabtree Publishing
386 Mt. Alexander Rd.
Ascot Vale (Melbourne)
VIC 3032

CONTENTS

FOOD FOR FUEL

People say you are what you eat, but you do not have carrots for arms and celery for legs. While it is important to eat a balanced diet of milk and dairy foods, meat or alternatives, fruits, vegetables, and grains, it is what is inside these foods that your body uses to stay alive and healthy.

Essential minerals

Your body is at work all the time—and it needs nutrients, including minerals, to carry out its daily tasks. Even when you are sleeping, your body is still working. Messages are being sent back and forth along your nerves to make muscles move so your lungs can breathe in oxygen from the air. **Enzymes** are breaking down food in your stomach. Your blood is delivering food and oxygen to your muscles and cells. None of these things are possible if you are not giving your body the **nutrients** it needs.

It is important to eat fruits to stay healthy. They are packed with essential vitamins and minerals.

The food pyramid shows healthy foods only. It does not include foods such as cookies and chips, which are high in salt, fat, or sugar.

Grains
Grains give you energy, but they also contain some protein and other nutrients.

Vegetables and fruits
You should eat a wide range from these two groups to get all the nutrients you need.

Oils and fats
These foods should not be overeaten.

Milk
This group of foods is rich in protein but can also be high in fat.

Meat and beans
These foods are rich in protein, although meats can also be high in fat.

You need nutrients

Your body needs large amounts of nutrients called carbohydrates, proteins, and fats to stay healthy. You also need tiny amounts of nutrients called vitamins and minerals. This book is about minerals.

You have to eat enough of each nutrient to stay healthy. Luckily, different nutrients are found in many foods, so you can choose healthy foods that you like.

WHAT ARE MINERALS?

Minerals are the elements that your body needs to work properly and stay healthy. Elements are basic building blocks from which everything is made, including plants and animals. Most of your body is made of four main elements. They are carbon, nitrogen, oxygen, and hydrogen. If you took all of those elements out of your body, you would be left only with dietary minerals, such as calcium and iron.

Body Talk

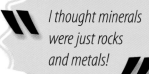

You often hear vitamins and minerals mentioned together. They are both micronutrients—things the body needs in tiny amounts to stay healthy.

I thought minerals were just rocks and metals!

You cannot chew on a piece of iron ore to get your daily iron supply!

Did you know?

Minerals are different from vitamins because they are not **organic**. Organic means coming from life. Vitamins are complex molecules that are built inside plants and animals. Minerals are much simpler molecules. They are not built by plants and animals. They come from the soil and water.

Dietary minerals are part of a healthy, balanced diet. Without iron, we could not move oxygen to our muscles. Without calcium, we could not have strong bones or teeth. Minerals such as iron and calcium help our bodies work and grow.

Mineral molecules

The many different minerals that we get from our food are too small to see. Minerals may be present as just a few atoms. Atoms are the tiny particles that make up everything in the world. Groups of atoms join together to form larger particles called **molecules**.

Atoms of the same type are called elements.
The chart below is called the periodic table.
It shows all the known elements.

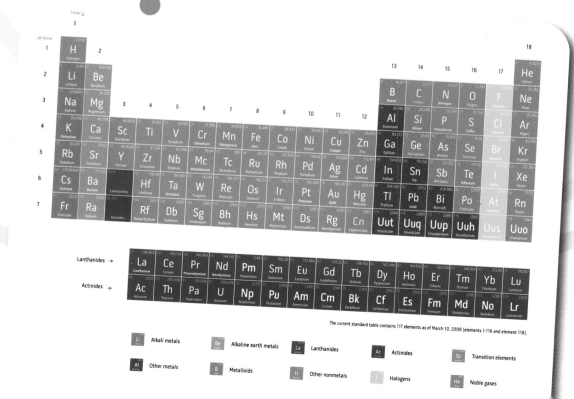

The current standard table contains 117 elements as of March 10, 2009 (elements 1-116 and element 118).

Li — Alkali metals
Be — Alkaline earth metals
La — Lanthanides
Ac — Actinides
Sc — Transition elements
Al — Other metals
B — Metalloids
H — Other nonmetals
I — Halogens
He — Noble gases

7

These cod liver oil capsules contain high levels of fatty acids and vitamins A and D. These nutrients help keep our joints healthy and improve the health of our bones and skin.

Macrominerals and microminerals

Without minerals, our bodies would not work. Even a small shortage of a mineral can cause problems. There are 15 minerals that are essential parts of our diet. Some, such as calcium and sodium, are needed in bigger quantities. These are called macrominerals. Others are needed in much smaller quantities but are still very important. These are called microminerals.

A lion's tale

People first began to learn how minerals affect the body in 1885 —at the London Zoo. Here, lion cubs were coming down with rickets —a softening of the bones caused by a lack of the mineral calcium and vitamin D. At that time, scientists had known about rickets for 250 years, but they did not know what caused the disease or how to treat it.

Call the doctor!

The London Zoo called in the best doctor in the city, John Bland-Sutton. He did not know what caused rickets either, but as a farmer's son, he guessed that the horsemeat the lion cubs ate did not contain enough fat.

The doctor told the zookeepers to feed the lions a mixture of ground-up bones and cod liver oil. These contain high levels of the minerals calcium and phosphorus. Within a few weeks, the lions were cured.

Body Talk

Scientists began to understand the role minerals play in the human body through experiments such as the one with the lions. By 1906, a scientist named Frederick Hopkins defined what minerals were and how they made the body work. Hopkins and other scientists showed that diseases such as beriberi in Asia and pellagra in Italy were not caused by germs, but diets lacking in vitamins and minerals.

Meat-eating lions need vitamins and minerals to stay healthy just as people do.

MINERALS ON THE MENU

How can you be sure that you are giving your body all the minerals it needs to stay healthy? The best answer is to eat a balanced diet. Eating a good balance of a wide variety of foods means you are more likely to get all the different minerals you need. It also keeps your meals from getting boring.

I used to have really bad acne until my doctor recommended that I use a cream that contains zinc. It is a great zit-buster!

Acne creams deliver zinc directly to the problem area.

Body Talk

The body can also absorb minerals through the skin. Certain medical creams are used to treat skin conditions such as **eczema**. Minerals that help the skin include zinc, which makes skin less **inflamed**.

Did you know?

Water flowing up from the ground from natural springs contains minerals dissolved from the rocks it flowed through. These minerals might be good for your health. Each natural spring is different. Some mineral water companies will add minerals to their water for their health benefits.

When animals eat plants or other animals, minerals pass from one organism to another through the food chain. They eventually make their way to our plates and our bodies.

How do minerals get into our food?

Minerals come from the soil. They are dissolved in water and are absorbed by plants through their roots. When we eat the plants, we eat the minerals they contain. Livestock, such as cows and sheep, also eat plants, so we take in minerals by eating meat, too. Which minerals appear in which plants and animals depends on the condition of the soil the plants were growing in. Our food will contain more minerals if we eat plants that have grown in healthy soil with plenty of minerals.

We are more likely to get calcium from dairy products because milk from mammals is rich in calcium. Milk contains calcium to help baby mammal bones grow strong.

Fortified foods

Sometimes it is not possible to get enough minerals just by eating the right foods. We can still get the minerals we need by **fortifying** the food we eat. Examples of fortified foods include breakfast cereals and table salt. Breakfast cereals are often fortified with iron. This metal mineral helps your blood carry oxygen around your body. Table salt is fortified with a mineral called iodine, which helps a gland in your neck, called the thyroid gland, make important **hormones** that keep your body healthy.

In some parts of the world water from the faucet is fortified with fluoride. This important mineral is needed to keep your teeth healthy.

Did you know?

Toothpaste contains fluoride, the mineral that helps to keep your tooth enamel strong and healthy.

Supplements are useful when people have problems with their diets or if their bodies process minerals in a different way. Supplements help people get the nutrients they need.

Taking supplements

Another way to deal with not having enough minerals in your diet is to take supplements. Unlike fortified foods, you have to take the supplements themselves, usually as a pill.

> *I take a daily supplement to keep myself healthy.*

Try this...

What you need:
1. 2 cups (475 ml) cereal (with 100% of the daily allowance of iron; check the label)
2. 1 cup (240 ml) water
3. A blender
4. A glass, ceramic, or plastic bowl (*not* metal!)
5. A strong magnet (stronger than an ordinary fridge magnet)

Instructions:
1. Take the cereal and blend it with the water for at least five minutes.
2. Pour the mixture into a glass, plastic, or ceramic bowl.
3. Move the magnet around in the mixture. Do this for a while.
4. Take the magnet out of the bowl and look at it. You will find black flecks attached to the magnet.

What just happened:
These are iron filings—bits of iron added to the cereal.
IMPORTANT: Iron is okay to eat in cereal form, but DO NOT eat it as iron filings.

HOW MUCH DO WE NEED?

It is important that you eat a balanced diet to get all of the proteins, carbohydrates, vitamins, and minerals your body needs. It is also important to get the balance right. Having too much or too little of certain minerals can upset the balance of your body and make you sick.

Body Talk

If you do not get enough magnesium, your nerves and muscles can stop working, and your heart can stop beating.

A healthy body is a happy body. Your body is in balance when you eat the right nutrients.

Have you ever found yourself feeling tired and weak? Do you get muscle cramps when you run around and play? Do your hands shake? You may not have gotten enough minerals for your body to work or you may have gotten too much.

Minerals and health

If you do not have enough of a certain mineral, the part of the body that uses that mineral stops working properly. This table shows you the names for the medical conditions caused by having too much or too little of certain minerals.

Mineral	Too Little	Too Much
Potassium	hypokalemia	hyperkalemia
Sodium	hyponatremia	hypernatremia
Calcium	hypocalcemia	hypercalcemia
Iron	anemia	hemochromatosis
Manganese	manganese deficiency	manganism
Iodine	iodine deficiency	iodism

Notice that the names of the medical conditions in the table give clues about what they mean. *Hyper*, as in "hyperactive," means too fast or too much. *Hypo*, as in "hypothermia," means too little or not enough.

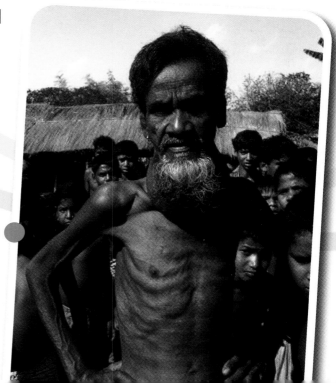

This man has a large swelling in his neck, called a goiter. This is a symptom of a lack of iodine in the diet.

Macrominerals

Your body needs a lot of some minerals. These are called the macrominerals. An average person needs more than 100 milligrams of macrominerals every day. The human body will also store more than 0.2 ounces (5 g) of these minerals in case you do not get enough in your food.

There are seven macrominerals:

Calcium is important for strong bones and teeth and healthy muscles.

Phosphorus works with calcium to build healthy bones and teeth. Phosphorus is also important in processing energy.

Potassium keeps muscles and nerves working properly.

Sulfur helps the body to break down carbohydrates, fats, and some vitamins. It is also used to make a hormone called insulin, the keratin that makes up your hair and fingernails, and the collagen that holds your body together.

Drinking milk is one of the best ways to get the calcium your body needs for healthy bones and teeth.

Sodium breaks down carbohydrates and protein in your digestive system and keeps minerals moving around the bloodstream. Sodium also helps your nerves to work properly.

Magnesium keeps your muscles and nerves working properly and your heart beating properly. Magnesium is also needed for strong bones and teeth and helps your immune system fight disease.

Chlorine helps your body make hormones and take in potassium from your food. This mineral is also needed to make hydrochloric acid, which helps your body break down food in the stomach.

The food pyramid shows which minerals are found in each food group. Chlorine is not shown but is easily obtained through salt. A child needs 1,900 mg per day.

I make sure I eat from every food group to get all the minerals I need.

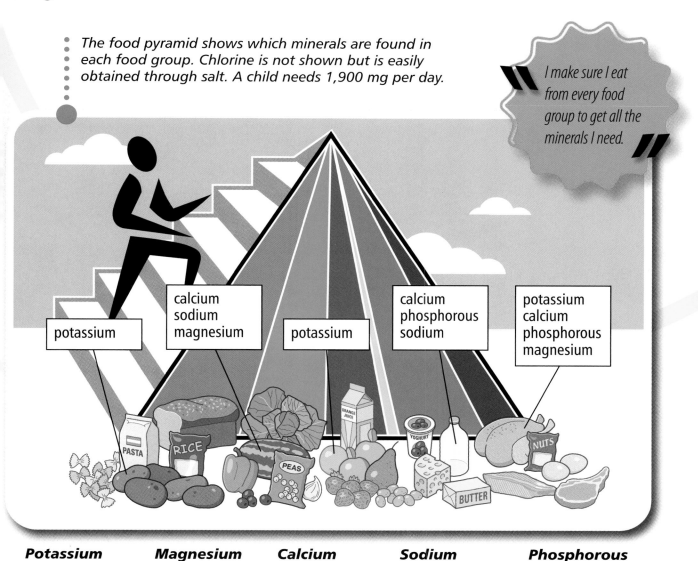

potassium

calcium
sodium
magnesium

potassium

calcium
phosphorous
sodium

potassium
calcium
phosphorous
magnesium

Potassium	**Magnesium**	**Calcium**	**Sodium**	**Phosphorous**
Child 9-13 needs 4,500 mg per day	*Child 9-13 needs 170 mg per day*	*Child 9-13 needs 800 mg per day*	*Child 9-13 needs 1,500 mg per day*	*Child 9-13 needs 800 mg per day*

Microminerals

Your body needs many more minerals in much smaller amounts. These are the so-called microminerals or trace minerals. While your body may only need very small amounts of trace minerals, the effects on the body can be huge.

Of all the trace minerals, these are the seven most important:

Iron is an important part of red blood cells. It is part of the chemical that red blood cells use to carry oxygen around the body. Extra iron is stored in your liver.

Zinc gives us healthy hair, skin, and nails. It also helps our body repair cuts and wounds and keeps our senses of smell and taste working.

Copper protects the heart from disease. This metal mineral also plays an important role in keeping your skin and hair in top condition.

Manganese is an **antioxidant**. It mops up free radicals–the harmful by-products of body processes–helping prevent cancer and heart disease. Manganese also helps the body convert protein and fat into energy.

Teenagers need to make sure they get enough minerals from their food because their bodies go through a lot of changes, including growth and puberty.

My doctor told me you cannot absorb iron unless you take vitamin C, too.

Selenium helps the body produce enzymes and disease-fighting cells called antibodies. Selenium also works with vitamin E as an antioxidant.

Molybdenum maintains the body's natural **pH** balance, making it neither too **acidic** nor too **alkaline**.

Molybdenum also helps the body make an enzyme that releases the iron stored in the liver.

Iodine helps the thyroid gland produce two important hormones that determine how fast and how efficiently the body burns calories.

iron
zinc
copper
selenium
molybdenum

iron
manganese
molybdenum
iodine

manganese

iron
zinc
copper
selenium
molybdenum
iodine

Iron	***Zinc***	***Copper***	***Manganese***	***Selenium***	***Molybdenum***	***Iodine***
Child 9-13 needs 10 mg per day	*Child 9-13 needs 10 mg per day*	*Child 9-13 needs 2 mg per day*	*Child 9-13 needs 3 mg per day*	*Child 9-13 needs 0.03 mg per day*	*Child 9-13 needs 0.022 mg per day*	*Child 9-13 needs 0.12 mg per day*

Snacks such as corn chips contain a lot of salt. Your body needs salt, but too much is bad for your health.

Too much or too little?

If you have too much of any mineral in your food, it can build up inside you and stop your body from working properly. One example is salt. Salt is sodium chloride—a chemical made up of the minerals sodium and chlorine. There is plenty of natural salt in food, but salt makes foods tastier. As a result, many people eat more salt than they need.

Body Talk

Your kidneys filter salt from your body, but they need lots of water to do this. This is why you feel thirsty after you have eaten a bag of salty potato chips. The extra water goes into your blood, which increases the amount of blood in your body. This increases blood pressure and can damage your kidneys, as well as lead to heart attacks and strokes.

Accidental sources

Sometimes people take too many mineral supplements. They think that if a mineral is good for you, more is better.

You can also get too much of a mineral by accident. In India, children got sick with a liver disease called cirrhosis. Their bodies had too much copper, which shut their livers down. The mineral came from food cooked in copper pots.

Other accidental sources include coming into contact with minerals at work. Welders get "welder's disease" or "zinc shakes" because they work with zinc and manganese every day.

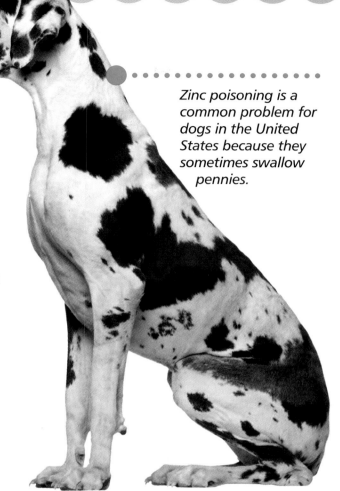

Zinc poisoning is a common problem for dogs in the United States because they sometimes swallow pennies.

I took too many supplements once, and it made me really sick.

Did you know?

Many people got sick from zinc poisoning when the U.S. mint started making its pennies out of copper-coated zinc. One man died after swallowing 425 pennies, which contained over 2.2 pounds (1 kg) of zinc.

21

Mineral deficiencies

If you do not have enough of a mineral in your body you can develop a **deficiency**. Over one third of the world is at risk of zinc deficiency because there is not enough zinc in the soil. The plants that grow in these soils lack zinc. People who eat the plants do not get all the zinc they need.

In 1993, an American research project added zinc to soil in Turkey. It improved the health of the children in the area.

Body Talk

Sweat removes salt as well as water from your body. This is why athletes drink sports drinks while working out, to restore the mineral balance in their bodies. If you are not exercising very hard you do not need to drink sports drinks, which also have a lot of sugar and calories.

A lack of iron can make you feel very tired.

Shutting down

In most cases, not having enough minerals in your body will make you slow down. You will feel tired and weak. In serious cases, your heart can stop beating. Some illnesses can cause your body to lose minerals. Diarrhea and vomiting remove essential nutrients from your body. Taking drugs and drinking too much alcohol can also lead to mineral deficiencies.

Try this...

Take a look at your eye in a mirror. Does the flesh inside the bottom lid look healthy and pink? If you lack iron, the color will be a much paler pink. When you have too much copper, deposits form a copper-colored ring around your pupil.

Sweating cools you down when playing sports. Take a sports drink with you to replace the nutrients you lose when you sweat.

My friend takes a mineral drink to the gym.

IT'S ON THE LABEL

Labels on food packaging also tell you how much of the **Recommended Daily Intake (RDI)** of each nutrient the food contains. This percentage is called the Daily Value (DV). For example, a label might say that a serving of four cookies contains 35 mg of sodium, which is a Daily Value of one percent of the RDI for sodium.

Many of the foods that people buy have a mixture of ingredients, and most ingredients have a mixture of nutrients. So how do you figure out how healthy or not a food is? The answer is on the label! The label tells you exactly what is in a food product and how much of each of the main nutrients and some important vitamins and minerals it contains.

I always read food labels when I go shopping. You need to know what you are eating or drinking.

Check the food labels to see which minerals are in the foods you buy to make sure you include a wide range of nutrients in your diet.

Did you know?

Bread provides us with many different minerals, but the most important is calcium, which helps build healthy bones and teeth. Bread also contains iron, which is essential for making blood. Other minerals present in smaller amounts include copper, magnesium, potassium, and sodium.

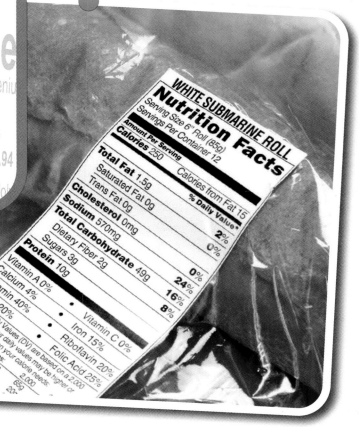

The nutrition label on this bread shows you how many nutrients the bread contains.

Start reading!

The next time you pick up a box of your favorite breakfast cereal take a closer look at the packaging. In North America, all foods must have a label on the packaging that tells you what nutrients the food contains. Minerals like iron, calcium, magnesium, and zinc are listed with the vitamins, carbohydrates, protein, and fat.

Using the labels

A label on a cereal box may give you the percentages based on a single cup (240 ml) of cereal. Of course, it is not accurate if you have two cups (475 ml) of cereal for your breakfast, and it does not count the nutrients you add when you pour in the milk or add a sprinkle of sugar.

MINERAL BODY BUILDERS

Body Talk

Calcium is the most common mineral in your body. Just over one percent of your body weight is calcium. If you weighed 110 pounds (50 kg), you would have 20 ounces (560 g) of calcium in your body.

Your body is a complicated machine. Messages must be sent from the brain along the nerves to make your muscles move. Things need to happen to process fuel and repair old cells, as well as make new cells to keep your skin, muscles, and bones growing. Many of these processes are due to chemical reactions. Minerals help these reactions occur.

Playing volleyball involves chemical reactions! You would not be able to play sports if your body did not have the nutrients it needs to make these reactions occur.

Did you know?

Here are all the elements that make up your body:

Oxygen (65%)
Carbon (18%)
Hydrogen (10%)
Nitrogen (3%)
Calcium (1.5%)
Phosphorus (1.0%)
Potassium (0.35%)
Sulfur (0.25%)
Sodium (0.15%)
Magnesium (0.05%)
Copper, Zinc, Selenium,
Molybdenum, Fluorine,
Chlorine, Iodine, Manganese,
Cobalt, Iron (0.70%)
Lithium, Strontium, Aluminum,
Silicon, Lead, Vanadium, Arsenic,
Bromine (trace amounts)

The green color in the leaves of plants comes from chlorophyll. Chlorophyll contains the mineral magnesium.

Making energy

All the minerals we get come from plants. Plants absorb minerals from the soil. When animals and people eat plants, they take in the minerals.

Animals and people rely on plants for their food. But plants make their own food in a process called photosynthesis.

During photosynthesis, a molecule called chlorophyll traps the energy from the sun. The energy converts the gas carbon dioxide from the air and water from the soil to make food for the plant to grow. When animals eat plants, they take the stored energy of the sun into themselves. Photosynthesis is important to all life on Earth.

Pumping iron

Your heart pumps blood to every part of the body. Blood carries oxygen from your lungs to all the different parts of your body. Cells need oxygen to change the food we eat into energy. Your blood also carries waste carbon dioxide back to the lungs. Your body gets rid of the carbon dioxide by breathing it back out. Without blood's constant movement, your body would stop working.

The most common blood cell is the red blood cell. These cells deliver oxygen to the different parts of your body. Red blood cells use a protein called hemoglobin to carry oxygen. Hemoglobin needs iron to do its job.

Body Talk

The human body contains up to 0.25 ounces (6 g) of iron, enough to make a small nail. Just under one half of this iron is in your blood. The rest is stored in your liver for future use.

Did you know?

Only 25 percent of the iron you eat gets used by your body. It is not easy absorbing iron into your body, and it cannot be done without vitamin C.

Without iron, red blood cells could not carry oxygen around the body. Iron is used to make the protein hemoglobin, which binds the oxygen to the red blood cells.

Not enough iron

If you do not have enough iron in your diet, your body cannot produce enough hemoglobin. This causes anemia, a condition where the body does not have enough red blood cells to transport oxygen to the parts of the body that need it. Not having enough oxygen leads to a condition called hypoxia, which can make you feel tired and weak. In serious cases of anemia your organs can stop working, causing death.

The white color of this child's inner eyelid is a sign that he is anemic.

Did you know?

We used to believe the red of blood was linked to iron, because it shared the color of rust. But it turns out iron has nothing to do with blood's red color—red is just the natural color of the hemoglobin protein.

Build it up

Bones do not start out hard. When babies are born, their bones are mostly made up of a soft, stringy tissue called **cartilage**. It takes a mineral called calcium to make bones into rigid structures that hold up the body. That is why babies need to drink a lot of calcium-rich milk. The calcium in the milk builds strong bones and teeth.

The enamel on teeth is the hardest substance in the human body. Tooth enamel cannot repair itself if it gets damaged. So it is important to get a lot of calcium when teeth

Body Talk

Bones can lose their density in a condition called **osteoporosis**. The bones get brittle and break much more easily. Getting enough calcium in your diet when you are growing will help prevent osteoporosis later.

Did you know?

Bones are where you will find 99 percent of your body's calcium, 75 percent of your body's phosphorus, and 50 percent of your body's magnesium.

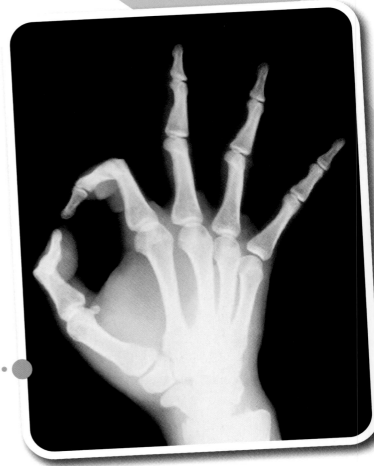

An X-ray reveals the bones that make up a human hand.

are forming, to make sure you will have them for a long time. That is another good reason to drink a lot of milk and eat calcium-rich dairy foods when you are growing up.

Too much calcium

Calcium is a vital mineral but too much can be dangerous. It causes **lethargy** and can give you very low blood pressure and an irregular heartbeat.

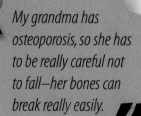

Eating calcium-rich foods, such as yogurt and cheese, helps to build strong and healthy teeth.

Try this...

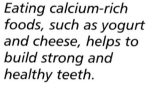
My grandma has osteoporosis, so she has to be really careful not to fall—her bones can break really easily.

What you need:
1. 1 chicken bone
2. A glass
3. White vinegar

Instructions:
1. Fill a glass with vinegar and place bone inside.
2. Check on the bone after a few weeks (replacing the vinegar as needed). You will notice that the bone has become flexible.

What just happened:
Calcium carbonate, the mineral that makes bones hard, dissolves in vinegar. With the calcium gone, all that is left in the bone is the cartilage it formed around.

DIGESTION

The digestive process starts as soon as you take a bite of food.

How do you turn the minerals in the food on your dinner plate into something you can use? You digest it!

The first step in the digestive process begins in your mouth. Your teeth cut up the food, and your tongue mixes in **saliva**. This produces a soft, mushy lump called a bolus. As you chew, enzymes in the saliva get to work, breaking up the food into smaller molecules.

Into the stomach

The tongue pushes the chewed food to the back of your mouth to be swallowed. Your food passes through your throat, down your **esophagus**, and into your stomach.

I chew my food thoroughly. It helps my body absorb minerals and vitamins.

The stomach's acid bath

Your stomach bathes the food in gastric acid produced by the wall of the stomach. The stomach also churns the food, mixing the food into a goopy soup called **chyme**. After a few hours, a valve at the bottom of the stomach opens to release some of this chyme into the small **intestine**.

Body Talk

On average, the food you eat stays inside your stomach for up to three hours.

The food you eat passes down the esophagus into the stomach. The partially digested food then moves to the small intestine.

Did you know?

It may sound gross, but your stomach is a breeding ground for microscopic bacteria. These tiny organisms are actually friendly because they help break down your food.

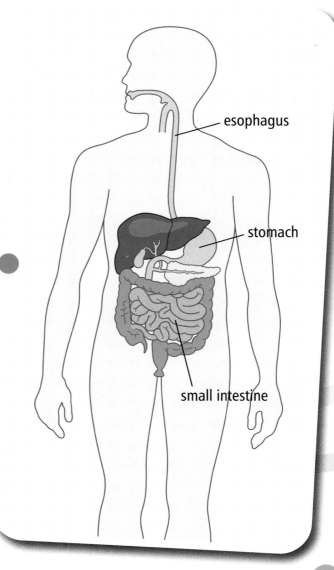

esophagus

stomach

small intestine

Some goes in, some goes out

The first section of the small intestine is called the duodenum. Here, chyme from the stomach is bathed in bile. This dark green liquid is produced by the liver and helps to break down any fats in the chyme. The chyme then moves into the rest of the small intestine, where the process of digestion continues.

Tiny fingerlike bumps, called villi, line the wall of the small intestine. This increases the surface area of the small intestine so that more nutrients and water can be absorbed into the bloodstream.

When you swim in the ocean, do not drink the salty water! Drinking seawater dehydrates you and makes you thirstier.

Did you know?

The small intestine of an average adult person is about 22 feet (7 m) long.

Body Talk

Your body removes any excess salt in your urine. But there is a limit to how much salt your body can remove. This is one reason why people cannot drink seawater. Seawater contains a lot of dissolved salt, so the kidneys have to work extra hard (and use more water) to remove the salt that you take in by drinking the seawater in the first place.

Body filters

Now that the minerals from your food are in your bloodstream, they are in a form that your body can use. The blood transports all the nutrients to every cell in the body, where they are used to provide fuel and carry out basic body processes. When your body has used all it can, your kidneys filter out any excess minerals, along with other waste products. This liquid waste leaves your body as **urine**.

Solid waste

We cannot digest everything in the food we eat. Any material that is not absorbed by the small intestine passes into the large intestine. This part of the digestive system is home to friendly bacteria that help digest what the small intestine cannot. The large intestine also absorbs as much water as it can. This makes the waste material more solid, before it finally leaves the body through your anus—the end of your digestive tract—as poop!

The gut-friendly bacteria in yogurt are good for your digestive system. They help to release the nutrients in your food.

MINERALS AND BODY SYSTEMS

Body Talk

Have you ever had a sudden muscle cramp in your legs? Cramps are usually harmless, but they hurt. Being short of minerals such as calcium, potassium, and magnesium can make you more likely to get these cramps.

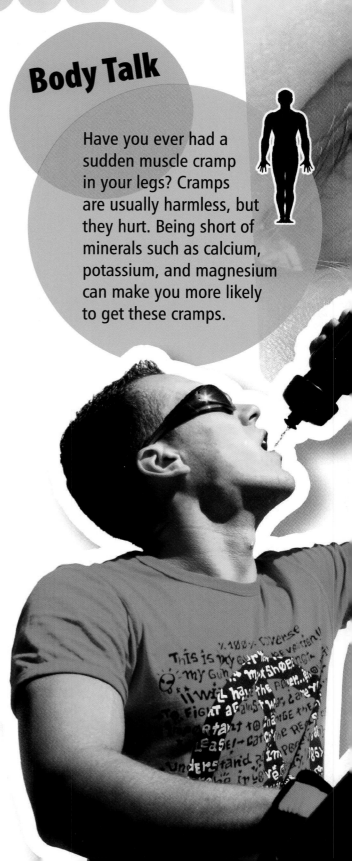

If your body is a machine, then your nerves are its electrical wiring. Your skin, tongue, ears, and eyes are the machine's sensors. These sensory organs send **impulses** along the nerves to report what they are feeling to the brain. Your brain is the control center of the body machine. The brain sends messages back and forth to all the different parts of the body, with instructions about what to do. Muscles also receive messages and are responsible for all the body's movements.

From touch to taste and sight, your body relies on minerals for all its senses.

> When I got cramps my doctor told me to eat more bananas. They are loaded with potassium.

When you exercise you lose electrolytes in your sweat. Many sports drinks contain electrolytes to replace those lost when you sweat.

Essential electrolytes

So how do you send these messages around your body? The answer is electrolytes. Electrolytes are atoms or groups of atoms called molecules that have an electric charge. Most electrolytes contain minerals such as calcium, chlorine, magnesium, and potassium. Without them, your brain would not know when your fingers were touching something hot. Your muscles would not respond by moving your hand away from the source of the heat. Hormones control the concentration of electrolytes in the body. Most of these hormones are made in the kidneys and adrenal gland.

Chemical messengers

Hormones are your body's messengers. They tell the body what to do and when. Hormones are chemicals made by special cells or groups of cells called glands. The blood carries these hormones to other parts of the body, where other cells **decode** their messages.

Hormones turn the body's processes on and off. For example, the adrenal gland releases a hormone called epinephrine in emergency situations. This hormone opens up arteries and airways, makes the heart beat faster, and gives the body more energy to respond.

Your body releases hormones when you feel stressed. This increases your heart rate and breathing rate and may make you feel depressed.

Did you know?

Puberty is a stage in life when you start to develop into an adult. Hormones kickstart the puberty process. Male hormones help the body to make sperm. Female hormones prepare the body for producing children.

Body Talk

The thyroid gland helps to control the body's energy levels. If your thyroid gland is not working well, you may feel tired, get headaches, or gain weight. Thyroid hormones contain the mineral iodine. The body also needs the minerals selenium and zinc to make use of the thyroid hormones.

Minerals, we need you!

Without dietary minerals, many of the body's hormones would stop working. Minerals like chromium, iodine, selenium, and zinc either help to make hormones, or help your body make use of them. For example, chromium helps a hormone called insulin to move sugar to where it is needed in the body. If you do not have enough chromium, sugar stays in your fat cells. This can lead to **diabetes**.

A doctor examines a patient's neck to check for thyroid problems that may be caused by a mineral deficiency.

Sharing the energy

Minerals are also important for building enzymes. These important substances speed up the chemical reactions that go on inside our bodies. For example, the body makes different types of digestive enzymes to break down our food. Lipases in stomach acid break down fatty foods, while amylases made by the pancreas and secreted, or carried, in our saliva help break down carbohydrates. A third group of digestive enzymes, called proteases, help our bodies digest proteins.

Body Talk

Most of the minerals we have looked at have been used by your body to make things happen. Minerals called antioxidants do the opposite. They can help to **counteract** the effects of harmful substances called free radicals, which cause heart disease, cancer, and other illnesses. The minerals manganese and selenium are often used as antioxidants.

The vital enzyme ATP delivers energy. Any activity, from sitting at a desk to dancing, would be impossible without it.

Magnificent magnesium

Magnesium is especially important. It is used by over 300 enzymes in the body, including adenosine triphosphate (ATP). ATP stores the energy the body has taken from food. This enzyme delivers that energy to cells throughout your body, which use it to grow or divide. ATP is like the body's battery; none of the cells in your body would function without it. Like many other minerals, the body needs only trace amounts of magnesium to work properly, but it plays a vital role in making sure that ATP and other enzymes work properly.

Keep your ATP battery charged up with leafy green vegetables such as cabbage. They are packed with magnesium.

Did you know?

The average human body uses and replaces about nine ounces (250 g) of ATP every day.

SPECIAL DIETS

Body Talk

Some people crave chocolate, but people who have a disease called pica crave nonfood items such as dirt. Young children and pregnant women are most likely to develop pica. Doctors think that this disease may be caused by an iron or zinc deficiency. Eating dirt is not a good idea because it can block your intestines.

The same diet does not work well for both kids and adults. Children need to eat a healthy balance of different foods to grow. As children develop into adults their bodies change and there are different nutritional needs.

Children

Children need the same basic nutrients as adults to stay healthy, but the amounts vary. For example, children need extra calcium to build strong bones and teeth and extra iron to supply the increasing volume of blood with hemoglobin. Teenage girls often need more iron during **puberty**, when they start to **menstruate**.

Pregnancy places a lot of nutritional demands on the expectant mother's body. Extra nutrients are needed to help build the baby's bones, muscles, and skin.

Pregnancy

Pregnant women need more minerals, too. They must eat foods rich in calcium, iron, magnesium, and phosphorous to support the baby developing in the uterus.

Growing older

As people grow older, they are more likely to develop a disease called osteoporosis. Their bones may lose density, or firmness, and become brittle and easy to break. The best way to prevent osteoporosis is to eat foods with plenty of calcium.

Did you know?

Osteoporosis affects more than 10 million people in the United States. About 80 percent of those affected are women.

One out of two women over the age of 50 will break a bone because of osteoporosis. Doctors say you should get regular exercise to prevent this condition in old age.

43

FOOD FACTS AND STATS

Since your body needs just small amounts of most minerals to function, very small measures are used, including milligrams (mg) and micrograms (μg). One thousand milligrams (or one million micrograms) is equal to one gram (g).

The quantities of minerals in different foods

Food	Minerals
1 cup (240 ml) of white beans	6.6 mg of iron
⅔ cup (160 ml) of raisins	2.1 mg of iron
1 cup (240 ml) of milk	300 mg of calcium, 247 mg of phosphorus
½ cup (120 ml) of ice cream	85 mg of calcium, 69 mg of phosphorus
½ cup (120 ml) of cashew nuts	72 mg of magnesium
1 baked potato with skin	55 mg of magnesium
1 slice of wholewheat bread	65 mg of phosphorus
1 banana	451 mg of potassium
1 cup (240 ml) of tomato juice	658 mg of potassium

Recommended daily amounts of nutrients for children age 9–13

Grains	5 oz (140 g) (girls) 6 oz (170 g) (boys)
Vegetables	2 cups(475 ml) (girls) 2.5 cups (600 ml) (boys)
Fruit	1.5 cups (350 ml)
Milk	3 cups (700 ml)
Meat and beans	5 oz (140 g)
Oils	5 teaspoons (25 ml)

Recommended daily amounts of various minerals

Mineral	Age 9–13	Male Age 19–24	Female Age 19–24	Male Age 25–50	Female Age 25–50
Boron	n/a	2 mg	2 mg	2 mg	2 mg
Calcium	800 mg	1200 mg	1200 mg	800 mg	800 mg
Chlorine	1900 mg	2300 mg	2300 mg	2300 mg	2300 mg
Chromium	0.015 mg	0.035 mg	0.025 mg	0.035 mg	0.025 mg
Copper	2 mg	3 mg	3 mg	3 mg	3 mg
Fluorine	3.2 mg	3.8 mg	3.1 mg	3.8 mg	3.1 mg
Iodine	0.12 mg	0.15 mg	0.15 mg	0.15 mg	0.15 mg
Iron	10 mg	10 mg	15 mg	10 mg	15 mg
Magnesium	170 mg	350 mg	280 mg	350 mg	280 mg
Manganese	3 mg	5 mg	5 mg	5 mg	5 mg
Molybdenum	0.022 mg	0.045 mg	0.045 mg	0.045 mg	0.045 mg
Phosphorus	800 mg	1200 mg	1200 mg	800 mg	800 mg
Potassium	4500 mg	4700 mg	4700 mg	4700 mg	4700 mg
Selenium	0.03 mg	0.07 mg	0.055 mg	0.07 mg	0.055 mg
Sodium	1500 mg	1500 mg	1500 mg	1500 mg	1500 mg
Vanadium	n/a	1 mg	1 mg	1 mg	1 mg
Zinc	10 mg	15 mg	12 mg	15 mg	12 mg

GLOSSARY

acidic Something that has the properties of an acid

alkaline Something that has the properties to neutralize an acid

antioxidant Mineral that mops up harmful products

cartilage Tough, flexible material

chyme Digestive juice

counteract To balance out

decode To figure something out

deficiency Lack of something

diabetes Disease in which the body lacks insulin

eczema Disease that results in itchy, flaky patches of skin

enzyme Protein that helps break down food in your system

esophagus Muscular tube that runs from your throat to your stomach

fortifying Adding elements to improve the quality of food

hormone Chemical released by cells or glands that controls processes in other parts of the body

impulse Message that triggers a reaction in the body

inflamed Red and sore

intestine Long tube in the body through which food passes after leaving the stomach

lethargy Without energy

menstruate When the lining of the uterus is discharged every month

molecule Smallest part of a substance

nutrient Healthy source of nourishment

organic Coming about naturally; coming from nature

osteoporosis Disease that causes bones to lose their density, or firmness

pH Measure of the acidity or alkalinity of a substance

puberty Phase of life when children's bodies change to become adults

Recommended Daily Intake (RDI) Set of guidelines for daily nutrition

saliva Watery mixture in the mouth

urine Liquid waste from the body

FURTHER READING

Further Reading

Sayer, Dr. Melissa, *Too Fat? Too Thin? The Healthy Eating Guidebook*.
Crabtree Publishing, 2009.

Doeden, Matt, *Eat Right*, Lerner, 2009.

Gardner, Robert, *Health Science Projects about Nutrition*.
Enslow Publishers, 2002.

Royston, Angela. *Vitamins and Minerals for a Healthy Body*.
Heinemann-Raintree, 2009.

Internet

Your Digestive System
http://kidshealth.org/kid/htbw/digestive_system.html

Learning about Minerals
http://kidshealth.org/kid/stay_healthy/
  food/minerals.html

Your Gross and Cool Body
http://yucky.discovery.com/flash/body/
  pg000126.html

Try this...

Consider keeping a food journal. Write down everything you eat for an entire week. What minerals did you eat? Were there any essential minerals missing from your diet?

INDEX